WESTERN EXPANSION:
Exploration and Settlement

edited by Cheryl Edwards

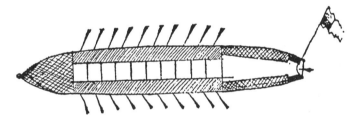

Clark's drawings of the Keelboat, Side Elevation, and Deck Plan.

© Discovery Enterprises, Ltd.
Lowell, Massachusetts
1995

© Discovery Enterprises, Ltd., Lowell, MA 1995
ISBN 1-878668-50-1 paperback edition
Library of Congress Catalog Card Number 94-69883

10 9 8 7 6 5 4 3 2

Printed in the United States of America

Subject Reference Guide

Westward Expansion: Exploration and Settlement
edited by Cheryl A. Edwards
Westward Expansion of the United States — Juvenile Literature
American History - Explorers, Settlers, Trappers,
Traders — Juvenile Literature
Lewis & Clark Expedition — Juvenile Literature
Daniel Boone — Juvenile Literature
Davy Crockett — Juvenile Literature
Sacajawea — Juvenile Literature

Photo/Illustration Credits

Map showing expansion of the U.S. (p. 7), from
The Louisiana Purchase and the Exploration Early History and Building of the West (Ginn and Co., The Athenaeum Press, 1904).

"Lewis & Clark Keelboat" (p. 24), photo by Sharon Niichel

"Sacajawea" (p. 28), redrawn by Jeff Pollock, based on a picture in *Sacajawea* by Olive Burt, (New York: Franklin Walts, 1978).

Map of Zebulon Pike's explorations (p. 36), from *The Boys Story of Zebulon M. Pike,* (New York: Charles Scribner's Sons, 1911).

"Daniel Boone" (p. 47), redrawn by Jeff Pollock, based on a picture of frontiers man from *Daniel Boone: Pioneer Trailblazer,* (Chicago: Childrens Press, 1985).

"The Crockett Almanacks" (p. 49), from *The Crockett Almanacks, Nashville Series, 1835-1838.*

Picture of flatboat (p. 57), from *The World's Great Explorers: Zebulon Pike,* (Chicago: Childrens Press, 1991).

Acknowledgments

Special thanks to Ron Williams of the Lewis & Clark State Park, Onawa, Iowa, for his assistance in putting together the graphics for this publication.

Table of Contents

Foreword
by
Cheryl Edwards

The indigenous people, often referred to as Indians or Native Americans, have lived throughout North America for thousands of years. American colonists, most of whom arrived on the east coast, have been moving westward ever since the Pilgrims arrived in the early 1600s. America's borders were constantly being pushed farther west as restless settlers looked for new opportunities and adventures on uncharted frontiers. The American colonists were not the only ones interested in the western lands. They had to compete for it with many Native American Nations whose ancestors had lived there for thousands of years before the European settlers arrived. The British, Spanish, and French staked their claims on various pieces of the western wilderness as well. It was not surprising that when all of these parties converged on the West, problems arose and tempers flared. The conflicts were troubling for a new country like the United States, and were to prove even more troubling to the Native Americans.

Before the American Revolution, the British forbade the colonists from settling west of the Appalachian Mountains. This artificial border, known as the Line of Proclamation, kept the British in control of the frontier. Many colonists ignored the British Proclamation of 1763 and moved westward into the forbidden land to settle. After the American Revolution ended in 1783, the land west of the Proclamation line, known as Ohio Country, became part of the United States. Beyond it was the uncharted wilderness, called Louisiana Province, which belonged to Spain.

Frontier settlement increased, and the idea of "going west" to seek their fortunes became the dream of many Americans. The desire for open space, better soil, cheap land, good hunting, and increased opportunities for trade made the West very appealing.

Frontiersmen like Daniel Boone and Davy Crockett helped open the Ohio Country for settlement by clearing trails and making crude roads through the mountains. Settlers who lived on the frontier used these trails to bring their families even further west and transport their trade goods to markets in the East. These trails were a slow, expensive, and inefficient way to travel. Americans needed an easier and cheaper way to transport their goods to market. Using waterways, like the Mississippi and Ohio Rivers, offered the best solution. Traders could ship their merchandise directly to the Port of New Orleans.

When the war between England and the United States ended in 1783, England promised the United States the right to free navigation on the Mississippi River. Spain controlled its mouth, and, at first, would not permit the Americans to drop off their trade goods at the Port of New Orleans. A volatile situation brewed.

In 1795, Spain and the United States signed a three-year treaty which permitted Americans to use the Mississippi River and deposit trade goods at the Port of New Orleans. Once that treaty had elapsed, Americans lost their right of deposit and difficulties between the two countries resumed.

President Jefferson wanted to avoid a war. The settlers who sailed the Mississippi were not going to let a foreign power dictate their right to use or not use the river. To further complicate matters, Spain gave the Louisiana Province to France in gratitude for its help in defeating the British. France was more powerful than Spain and presented a more serious threat to the United

States. However, France's Emperor, Napoleon, was busy
waging battles for the control of the European continent. He
did not have the time or sufficient money to defend his North
American colonies.

In addition to the problems he faced with France, Jefferson
had other concerns. He worried about the Americans who were
moving west in great numbers. The settlers needed a system
of law enforcement and protection from any potentially hostile
Native American nations or foreign governments. Jefferson
envisioned the borders of the United States extending across the
continent from the Atlantic to the Pacific coasts. He wanted to
unify the entire continent to take advantage of the economic pos-
sibilities in the West. Most importantly, Jefferson did not want
the continued presence of foreign powers on the continent. As a
sharp politician and negotiator, he knew what needed to be done
to save the United States from going to war again.

*Map showing the expansion of the United States, omitting
Alaska and Hawaii.*

In 1803, the United States negotiated the purchase of the western lands known as Louisiana Province from France for 15 million dollars. Jefferson's foresight and courage helped the country avoid a war, double its size, and secure important waterways that would make economic expansion possible. Although critics accused him of buying a useless piece of empty wilderness and wasting money, the President was resolute.

Jefferson had to show the skeptics that the Louisiana Purchase would be a valuable asset. Americans knew very little about their new acquisition. In 1804, Jefferson commissioned two army officers named Merriwether Lewis and William Clark to explore the newly-acquired western land. Jefferson was particularly interested in finding a good water route to the Pacific Ocean. Americans would then be able to trade more easily with countries in Asia.

Lewis and Clark's mission was to explore the Missouri and Columbia Rivers, record data about the flora and fauna, make friends with the Native Americans, and find an intercontinental route to the Pacific Ocean. Their twenty-eight month expedition included a group of men who were called the "Corps of Discovery." These men were specially trained to live in the wilderness. Also included in the expedition were a Shoshone woman named Sacajawea, her baby son Pomp, and her French husband Charbonneau. Clark's slave, named York, also came along. York was popular with the Native Americans, who had never seen a black man before. Through the journals of Lewis and Clark, we know that York had a great sense of humor. He told the Native Americans he met that he was a wild animal who had been tamed by Clark. When the expedition was complete, Clark freed York from slavery, out of respect for him and for his contribution to the success of the journey.

Lewis and Clark's expedition was a model undertaking. Other explorers soon followed, and new western lands were mapped and new trails opened. The rivers became busy with boats filled with goods for trading. Finally, the western lands were ready for settlement. Jefferson had proven his critics wrong: the natural resources and economic opportunities found in the West were magnificent.

Historians use many different methods to piece together events that happened in the past. They use primary sources such as diaries, journals, letters, photos, maps, drawings, autobiographies, oral histories, and interviews. Primary sources give historians a first person account of the event. Historians also use secondary sources such as textbooks, magazines, and newspaper articles. These are based on primary sources and give the reader the historian's analysis of the period or event.

In this book, I have used both primary and secondary sources to tell the story of America's westward expansion. I begin with Ripley Hitchcock's secondary source account of the Louisiana Purchase, written in 1903. I include journal excerpts from the explorers Lewis and Clark, Zebulon Pike, and both primary and secondary source documents about Sacajawea, Davy Crockett, Daniel Boone, fur traders, and daily life on the frontier.

Note: The words in the journal excerpts contain the original spelling. They have not been changed, even though much of the spelling is incorrect, or is based on old rules that are now considered out of date.

The Louisiana Purchase

Excerpt from *The Louisiana Purchase and the Exploration Early History and Building of the West.* By Ripley Hitchcock.

Source: Ripley Hitchcock, *The Louisiana Purchase and the Exploration Early History and Building of the West.* (Boston: Ginn and Co., The Athenaeum Press, 1904), pp. 3-7, 47-52, 226-229.

At the opening of the year 1803 the territory of the United States was bounded on the west by the Mississippi River. In April of that year a treaty was signed in Paris by which nearly a million square miles west of the river to British America, was purchased from France for $15,000,000, and the total area of country was more than doubled. This great event is known in history as the Louisiana Purchase. By this treaty ... the Republic of France ... ceded to the United States the territory which now contains Louisiana, Arkansas, Kansas, Missouri, Iowa, Nebraska, South Dakota, North Dakota, Montana, Wyoming, Indian Territory, and parts of Colorado and Oklahoma.

It is easy now to see that this great addition to our country was of incalculable importance. At the time, however, the significance of the purchase, which has been called a turning point in our history, was not realized. We can understand the situation better by showing what had been learned up to 1803 of the vast region which Jefferson and Napoleon added to the United States.

It is sometimes said that the Louisiana territory was unexplored. In one sense this is true, but we shall find that as a matter of fact many white men had penetrated this wilderness. The first were Spaniards who followed after Columbus. The purpose of Columbus, and, for a time, of others after him, was to find a water way to Cathay, or China, and the Spice Islands by the westward route, and to secure their rich trade. The extent of America was so little understood that much time was spent in trying to find a passage through or around our continent. Cipango, as Japan was called, was supposed to lie much farther east; indeed, in some old maps it seems included within our boundaries. It was the Spanish pioneer explorers of the sixteenth century who first penetrated western North America and discovered the vast extent of our country.

....

Up to the end of the Revolution the possession of Louisiana territory by one foreign power or another had not touched Americans closely. But now the conditions were changed. In the western migration of the later eighteenth century and the demands of these frontiersmen for a free route to the seaboard lay influences which finally resulted in the acquisition of Louisiana.

The growth of this movement is shown by the returns of the census for Kentucky, Tennessee, and the Northwest Territory, which then represented our West. In 1790 there were 73,677 people in Kentucky, and in 1800 there were 220,995. Tennessee showed 35,691 people in 1790, and 105,602 in 1800. The census of 1790 gives no population for Ohio and Indiana territories, but ten years later there were 44,678. Before these stalwart pioneers the forests were swept aside to make room for farms. Rude log cabins were built with chimneys of logs plastered with mud. The settlers made their simple furniture with their own tools. Their hunting shirts and trousers were of homemade linsey, a mixture of linen and wool, and of deerskin. Most of their food was gained by their rifles and their traps. Corn was pounded or ground in rude stone mortars to make meal. But the vigor and energy of these hardy pioneers soon bettered their condition. They began to raise tobacco and wheat and to cure hams and bacon. Then came the question of trade.

How could they exchange these products for money or for goods of which they stood in need? There was no market at hand. The railroad was yet in the future. To the eastward lay the Alleghenies and a long and difficult journey by land impossible for their purposes. Their easiest and cheapest route to a market was by water, and close at hand were the Ohio and other rivers flowing to the Mississippi, and offering a tempting water way to New Orleans and the sea. But New Orleans was held by the Spaniards. Their laws and customs regulations were arbitrary; their business methods were antiquated, complicated, and irksome. Between their mediaeval rule and the free and impatient spirit of the pioneers there was instant conflict. In the early nineties the Spanish authorities closed navigation and refused to grant the right to deposit goods at New Orleans to await the arrival of trading vessels. This right was essential for the men who journeyed down the great river in their "broad-horns," or rude homemade boats.

A crisis seemed at hand in 1795, but it was averted by the Spanish minister of state, Manuel Godoy, known as the "Prince of Peace," who more than once had proved his friendly feeling for the United States. In 1795 a treaty was signed, which granted the right of deposit, with certain minor limitations, for three years. Thus an outbreak was averted. The way to a market was kept open during the three years, and thereafter until 1802. Then the Spaniards withdrew the right of deposit, the West rose in protest, and therein lay a potent motive for the acquisition of at least the mouth of the Mississippi. But the immediate demand of these American settlers was not for Louisiana, but simply for an open seaport, or at most the possession of the river's mouth.

12

The Lewis and Clark Expedition

Excerpt from the letter written by Thomas Jefferson to Lewis and Clark. The letter contains instructions for their expedition in 1803.

Source: Thomas Jefferson. *Thomas Jefferson - Writings* (The Library of America), pp. 1127, 1129-1131.

... the object of your mission is to explore the Missouri river, & such principal stream of it, as, by it's course & communication with the water of the Pacific Ocean may offer the most direct & practicable water communication across the continent, for the purposes of commerce.

Beginning at the mouth of the Missouri, you will take observations of latitude and longitude at all remarkable points on the river, & especially at the mouths of rivers, at rapids, at marks & characters of a durable kind, as that they may with certainty be recognized hereafter. The courses of the river between these points of observations may be supplied by the compass, the log-line & by time, corrected by the observations themselves. The variations of the compass too, in different places should be noticed.

The interesting points of the portage between the heads of the Missouri & the water offering the best communication with the Pacific Ocean should be fixed by observation & the course of that water to the ocean, in the same manner as that of the Missouri.

Your observations are to be taken with great pains & accuracy, to be entered distinctly, & intelligibly for others as well as yourself, to comprehend all the elements necessary, with the aid of the usual tables to fix the latitude & longitude of the places at which they were taken, & are to be rendered to the war office, for the purpose of having the calculations made concurrently by proper persons within the U.S. Several copies of these as well as of your other notes, should be made at leisure times & put into the care of the most trustworthy of your attendants, to guard by multiplying them against the accidental losses to which they will be exposed. A further guard would be that one of these copies be written on the paper of the birch, as less liable to injury from damp than common paper.

Thomas Jefferson

The commerce which may be carried on with the people inhabiting the line you will pursue, renders a knolege of these people important. You will therefore endeavor to make yourself acquainted, as far as a diligent pursuit of your journey shall admit.

with the names of the nations & their numbers;

the extent & limits of their possessions;

their relations with other tribes or nations;

their language, traditions, monuments;

their ordinary occupations in agriculture, fishing, hunting, war, arts, & the implements for these;

their food, clothing, & domestic accommodations;

the diseases prevalent among them, & the remedies they use;

moral and physical circumstance which distinguish them from the tribes they know;

peculiarities in their laws, customs & dispositions;

and articles of commerce they may need or furnish & to what extent.

Other objects worthy of notice will be

the soil & face of the country, its growth & vegetable productions; especially those not of the U.S.

animals of the country generally, & especially those not known in the U.S.

The remains & accounts of any which may be deemed rare or extinct;

the mineral productions of every kind; but more particularly metals, limestone, pit coal & saltpetre; salines & mineral waters, noting the temperature of the last & such circumstances as may indicate their character; volcanic appearances;

climate as characterized by the thermometer, by the proportion of rainy, cloudy & clear days, by lightening, hail,

snow, ice, by the access & recess of frost, by the winds,
prevailing at different seasons, the dates at which particular
plants put forth or lose their flowers, or leaf, times of
appearance of particular birds, reptiles or insects.

In all your intercourse with the natives treat them in the
most friendly & conciliatory manner which their own conduct
will admit; allay all jealousies as to the object of your journey,
satisfy them of it's innocence, make them acquainted with the
position, extent, character, peaceable & commercial dispositions
of the U.S., of our wish to be neighborly, friendly & useful to
them, & of our dispositions to a commercial intercourse with
them; confer with them on the points most convenient as mutual
emporiums, & the articles of most desirable interchange for them
& us. If a few of their influential chiefs, within practicable distance, wish to visit us, arrange such a visit with them, and furnish them with authority to call on our officers, on their entering
the U.S. to have them conveyed to this place at the public ex-
pense. If any of them should wish to have some of their young
people brought up with us, & taught such arts as may be useful to them, we will receive, instruct & take care of them. Such
a mission, whether of influential chiefs, or of young people,
would give some security to your own party. Carry with you
some matter of the kine-pox, inform those of them with whom
you may be of it's efficacy as a preservative from the small-pox;
and instruct & encourage them in the use of it...

Should you reach the Pacific Ocean inform yourself of the
circumstances which may decide whether the furs of those parts
may not be collected as advantageously at the head of the Missouri (convenient as is supposed to the waters of the Colorado &

Oregon or Columbia) as at Nootka Sound or any other point of that coast; & that trade be consequently conducted through the Missouri & U.S. more beneficially than by the circumnavigation now practised.

On your arrival on that coast endeavor to learn if there be any port within your reach frequented by the sea-vessels of any nation, and to send two of your trusted people back by sea, in such way as shall appear practicable, with a copy of your notes. And should you be of the opinion that the return of your party by the way they went will be eminently dangerous, then ship the whole, & return by sea by way of Cape Horn or the Cape of Good Hope, as you shall be able. As you will be without money, clothes or provisions, you must endeavor to use the credit of the U.S. to obtain them; for which purpose open letters of credit shall be furnished you authorizing you to draw on the Executive of the U.S. or nay of its officers in any part of the world, in which drafts can be disposed of, and to apply with our recommendations to the consuls, agents, merchants or citizens of any nation with which we have intercourse, assuring them in our name that any aids they may furnish you, shall be honorably repaid and on demand...

The Journals of Lewis and Clark

*The following excerpts contain information on exploration
of the Missouri and Columbia Rivers, flora and fauna, Native
Americans, life on the expedition, and a description of the discovery of a intercontinental route to the Pacific Ocean.*

Source: Bernard DeVoto, ed. *The Journals of Lewis and Clark.* (Boston:
Houghton Mifflin Company, The Riverside Press Cambridge, 1953), pp. 94-95,
267-268, 286-288.

[Lewis]   Saturday April 13th

The wind was in our favour after 9 A.M. and continued
favourable untill three 3. P.M. we therefore hoisted both the sails
in the White Perogue, consisting of a small squar sail, and spritsail, which carried her at a pretty good gate, untill about 2 in the
afternoon when a sudden squall of wind struck us and turned the
perogue so much on the side as to allarm Sharbono who was
steering at the time, in this state of alarm he threw the perogue
with her side to the wind, when the spritsail gibing was as near
overseting the perogue as it was possible to have missed. the
wind however abating for an instant I ordered Drewyer to the
helm and the sails to be taken in, which was instant executed
and the perogue being steered before the wind was agin plased in
a state of security. this accedent was very near costing us dearly.
beleiving this vessell to be the most steady and safe, we had
embarked on board of it our instruments, Papers, medicine and
the most valuable part of the merchandize which we had still
in reserve as presents for the Indians. we had also embarked
on board ourselves, with three men who could not swim and the
squaw with the young child, all of whom, had the perogue over-
set, would most probably have perished, as the waves were high,

18

and the perogue upwards of 200 yards from the nearest shore; just above the entrance of the little Missouri the great Missouri is upwards of a mile in width, tho' immediately at the entrance of the former it is not more than 200 yards wide and so shallow that the canoes passed it with seting poles.

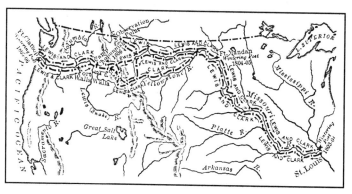

Map of Lewis and Clark expedition

we found a number of carcases of the Buffaloe lying along shore, which had been drowned by falling through the ice in winter and lodged on shore by the high water when the river broke up about the first of this month. we saw also many tracks of the white bear of enormous size, along the river shore and about the carcases of the Buffaloe, on which I presume they feed. we have not yet seen one of these animals, tho' their tracks are so abundant and recent. the men as well as ourselves are anxious to meet with some of these bear. the Indians give a very formidable account of the strenth and ferocity of this anamal, which they never dare to attack but in parties of six eight or ten persons; and are even then frequently defeated with the loss of one or more of their party. the savages attack this animal with their bows and arrows and the indifferent guns with which the traders furnish them, with these they shoot with such uncertainty and at so short a distance, that (unless shot thro' head or heart wound not mortal) they frequently mis their aim & fall a sacrefice to the bear. this anamall is said more frequently to attack a man on meeting with him, than to flee from him. When the Indians are about to go in quest of the white bear, previous to their departure, they paint themselves and perform all those supersticious rights commonly observed when they are about to make war uppon a neighbouring nation. Oserved more bald eagles on this part of the Missouri

One of Lewis's journal pages,
with his drawing of a bird

than we have previously seen. saw the small hawk, frequently called the sparrow hawk, which is common to most parts of the U. States. great quantities of gees are seen feeding in the praries. saw a large flock of white brant or gees with black wings pass up the river; there were a number of gray brant with them.

....

[Clark]   October 28th Monday 1805

A cool windey morning we loaded our canoes and Set out at
9 oClock, a.m. as we were about to set out 3 canoes from above
and 2 from below came to view us in one of those canoes I
observed an Indian with round hat Jacket & wore his hair cued
we proceeded on at four miles we landed at a Village of 8 houses
on the Stard. Side under some rugid rocks, I entered one of the
houses in which I saw a British musket, a cutlash and Several
brass Tea kittles of which they appeared verry fond Saw them
boiling fish in baskets with Stones, here we purchased five
Small Dogs, Some dried buries, & white bread made of roots,
the wind rose and we were obliged to lie by all day at 1 mile
below on the Lard Side. we had not been long on Shore before
a Canoe came up with a man woman & 2 children, who had a
fiew roots to Sell, Soon after many others joined them from
above, The wind which is the cause of our delay, does not retard
the motions of those people at all, as their canoes are calculated
to ride the highest waves, they are built of white cedar or Pine
verry light wide in the middle and tapers at each end, with aperns,
and heads of animals carved on the bow, which is generally
raised. wind blew hard accompanied with rain all the evening,
our Situation not a verry good one for an encampment, but such
as it is we are obliged to put up with, the harbor I s a Safe one,
we encamped on the Sand, wet and disagreeable.

....

                              November 18th Monday 1805

I set out with 10 men and my man York to the Ocean by
land. i.e. Serjt. Ordway & Pryor, Jos. & Ru Fields, Go. Shan-
non, W. Brattin, J. Colter, P. Wiser, W. Labieche & P. Shabono
one of our interpreters & York. I set out at Day light and proceeded on a Sandy beech

after dinner to a Small rock island in a deep nitch passed a nitch in which there is a dreen from Some ponds back; the land low opposite this nitch a bluff of yellow clay and Soft Stone from the river to the commencement of this nitch. below the countrey rises to high hills of about 80 or 90 feet above the water. at 3 miles passed a nitch. this rock Island is Small and at the South of a deep bend in which the nativs inform us the Ships anchor, and from whence they receive their goods in return for their peltries and Elk skins &c. this appears to be a very good harber for large Ships. here I found Capt. Lewis name on a tree. I also engraved my name, & by land the day of the month and year, as also Several of the men.

to the iner extremity of *Cape Disapointment* passing a nitch in which there is a Small rock island, a Small Stream falls into this nitch from a pond which is imediately on the Sea coast passing through a low isthmus. this Cape is an ellivated circlier [cir-]cular] point covered with thick timber on the iner Side and open grassey exposure next to the Sea and rises with a Steep assent to the hight of about 150 or 160 feet above the leavel of the water this cape as also the Shore both on the Bay & Sea coast is a dark brown rock. I crossed the neck of Land low and ½ of a mile wide to the main ocian, at the foot of a high open hill projecting into the ocian, and about one mile in Si[r]cumfrance. I assended this hill which is covered with high corse grass. decended to the N. of it and camped. [walked] 19 Miles [to-day].

from Cape Disapointment to a high point of a Mount which we shall call [*Clarke's Point of View*] beares S. 20°W. about 40 [25] miles, point adams is verry low and is Situated within the derection between those two high points of land, the water appears verry Shole from off the mouth of the river for a great distance, and I cannot assertain the direction of the deepest chanel,

22

the Indians point nearest the opposit Side. the waves appear to
brake with tremendous force in every direction quite across a
large Sand bar lies within the mouth nearest to point Adams
which is nearly covered at high tide. men appear much Satisfied
with their trip beholding with estonishment the high waves dash-
ing against the rocks & this emence Ocian

....

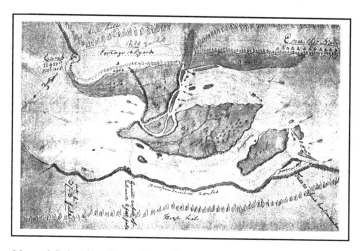

Map of Columbia River drawn by Clark

November the 19th 1805.
    I arose early this morning from under a Wet blanket caused
by a Shower of rain which fell in the latter part of the last night,
and Sent two men on a head with directions to proceed on near
the Sea Coast and Kill Something for brackfast and that I should
follow my self in about half an hour. after drying our blankets a
little I set out with a view to proceed near the Coast the direction
of which induced me to conclude that at the distance of 8 or 10
miles, the Bay was at no great distance across. I overtook the
hunters at about 3 miles, they had killed a Small Deer on which

we brackfast[ed], it Comen[c]ed raining and continued moderately untill 11 oClock A M.

after taking a Sumptious brackfast of Venison which was roasted on Stiks exposed to the fire, I proceeded on through ruged Country of high hills and Steep hollers to the commencement of a Sandy coast which extended to a point of high land distant near 20 miles. this point I have taken the Liberty of Calling after my particular friend Lewis. at the commencement of this Sand beech the high lands leave the Sea Coast in a Direction to Chinnook river, and does not touch the Sea Coast again below point Lewis leaveing a low pondey Countrey, maney places open with small ponds in which there is great numbr. of fowl I am informed that the *Chinnook* Nation inhabit this low country and live in large wood houses on a river which passes through this bottom Parrilal to the Sea coast and falls into the Bay

Lewis & Clark Keelboat — Replica of the boat central to the Lewis & Clark Expedition in 1804.

I proceeded on the sandy coast and marked my name on a Small pine, the Day of the month & year, &c. and returned to the foot of the hill, I saw a Sturgeon which had been thrown on Shore and left by the tide 10 feet in length, and Several joints of the back bone of a Whale, which must have foundered on this part of the Coast. after Dineing on the remains of our Small Deer I proceeded to the bay distance about 2 miles, thence up to the mouth of Chinnook river 2 miles, crossed this little river in the Canoe we left at its mouth and Encamped on the upper Side in any open sandy bottom.

Sacajawea: Scout for Lewis and Clark

Much has been written about Sacajawea, the Shoshone woman who served as a scout for Lewis and Clark. In the following story, Cheryl Edwards interprets history with a fictionalized account, written from Sacajawea's viewpoint, of how she came to be their scout.

Sacajawea's Story
by
Cheryl Edwards

My name is Sacajawea. I am a Shoshone woman. I once lived in the big mountains with my family and other members of the Snake people community. The men of my community liked to hunt buffalo down on the plains. There were enough buffalo there for many hunters to kill. However, the people who lived near the plains became angry with the Snake people. They wanted all the buffalo for themselves and did not like any outsiders to hunt near their villages.

When I was eleven years old, the plains people raided our village in retaliation. I was kidnapped and taken (more than 600 miles away from my home) to the village of the Mandan and the Minatree people, who lived by the banks of the Missouri River. I became a slave. I worked hard and I did everything my Minatree family asked me to do. Yet, I thought of my family day and night, and longed to see them again.

One day, a French trader named Toussaint Charbonneau came to the Mandan village. He played card games with members of the village, and he won. My Minatree family had to give me to Charbonneau as payment for their debt in gambling. Charbonneau took me as his wife.

In the winter of 1804, an unexpected turn of events changed my life. Two white men named Lewis and Clark came to our village. They were going on a long journey westward for their Great Chief. The journey would take them across the big mountains to the home of the Snake people. They needed to bring a guide and a Shoshone interpreter to help them. My husband Charbonneau accepted the white men's offer. All that winter in the Mandan Village, I dreamt that I would finally have a chance to go back to my people. During that time, I gave birth to a baby boy named Pomp. In the spring, when I was sixteen years old, we began our journey.

We travelled by foot, on horseback, and by boat. The white men had strange ideas about travel. They took along many unnecessary things that weighed them down and made travel difficult and slow. The white men also had a dangerous custom of building large fires at night that could alert the enemy and provoke an unexpected attack. I told them that they should be more careful, but they laughed at me. They told me not to worry because they had powerful guns for protection.

My baby son Pomp was my first concern. He was only a tiny baby of two months when we began our trip. I carried him on my back and stopped to feed and wash him when he was hungry. The white men would often complain about climbing steep mountains and navigating rough waters. I would laugh to myself about their silly complaints. I did all these things while carrying a squirming, heavy child. As Pomp grew, I could no longer carry him on my back. I carried him in front wrapped in a large blanket. This would often throw me off balance when climbing steep rocky hills.

27

Sacajawea

Once, while we were floating down a river, our boat capsized. Everyone fell overboard as well as our supplies and the white men's precious papers. I swam to the shore with Pomp on my back. I then swam back to retrieve the lost supplies. The men were grateful.

Our journey was long and arduous, but the white men found many new trails and places of interest for their Chief. We sailed great rivers and finally reached the Everywhere-Salt-Water. Along the way, I found my people and had a joyous reunion. The Shoshone man I had been promised to in marriage did not claim me when he saw Pomp. I could never have seen my family again without the kindness of the white men, Lewis and Clark.

The next spring and summer, I led Clark back, travelling by raft on the Yellowstone and Missouri Rivers. Where the rivers joined, we met up with Lewis and together returned to the Mandan village. When our journey ended, Lewis and Clark gave me a beautiful medal, which I always wear around my neck. The medal reminds me of the many journeys in my life.

This excerpt is from Sacajawea's actual autobiography. She told her life story in her own words to James Willard Schultz. Sacajawea's skills and insight turned out to be an invaluable asset to the expedition.

Source: James Willard Schultz. *Bird Woman.* (Boston: Houghton Mifflin Company, The Riverside Press Cambridge, 1918), pp. 141-144.

Upon my man's return to the fort the boats were all loaded. We had two large ones and six small ones, and we abandoned the fort and headed up the river. At the same time that we started, Long Knife and Red Hair sent their very large boat down the river in charge of some of their men. It was loaded with many skins, bones, and other things, presents for the great chief of the whites. Counting in my son, we were thirty-three people in our eight boats. I was given a place in one of the two large ones.

As we went on and on up the river, sometimes making a long distance between the rising and the setting of the sun, I was, at times, I believe, happier than I had ever been in my life, for each day's travel brought me so much nearer my people whom I so much longed to see. Then at other times, whenever I thought of what was before us, I would become very unhappy. I would say to myself that we could not possibly survive the dangers we should be sure to encounter along the way. I may as well say it: my good, kind white chiefs were not cautious; they were too brave, too sure of themselves. From the very start they and their men would foolishly risk their lives by attacking all the man-killing bears that came in sight of us. At night they would build great fires and would be sure to attract to us any wandering war party that might be in the country. After we passed the mouth of the Yellowstone and entered the country of the Blackfeet, I begged my chiefs to be more cautious. I asked them to stop always a short time before dark and build little cooking-fires, and then, after our meal, to put out the fires, and then go on until dark and make camp in the darkness. But they only laughed at me, and answered: "We have good guns and know how to use them."

I often said to myself: "Strange are these white men! Strange their ways! They have a certain thing to do, to make a trail to the west to the Everywhere-Salt-Water. Why, then, are we not on horseback and traveling fast and far each day? Here we are in boats, heavily loaded with all kinds of useless things, and when the wind is bad or the water swift, we make but little distance between sun and sun! We could have got all the horses that we needed from the Earth House tribes, and had we done that, we should long since have arrived at the mountains. Yes, right now I should probably be talking with my own people!"

And those medicine packages of theirs, packages big and little piled all around me in the boat in which I rode, how my chiefs valued them! One day a sudden hard wind struck our sail and the boat began to tip and fill with water. More and more it filled, and the men in it and those on the shore went almost crazy with fear. But I was not afraid. Why should I be when I knew that I could cast off my robe and swim ashore with my little son?

30

More and more water poured into the boat and the medicine packages began to float out of it. I seized them one by one as they were going, and kept seizing them and holding them, and when, at last, we reached the shore, my good white chiefs acted as though I had done a wonderful thing in saving their packages; it seemed as though they could not thank me enough for what I had done. Thinking about it, after it was all over, and when the things had been spread out to dry, I said to myself: "Although I cannot understand them, these little instruments of shining steel and these writings on thin white paper must be powerful medicine. Hereafter, whenever we run into danger, I shall, after my son, have my first thought for their safety, and so please my kind white chiefs."

After leaving the mouth of Little River, or, as my white chiefs named it, Milk River, we went up through a part of the Big River Valley that I had not seen, for, when I was captured by the Minnetarees, we had, after leaving the valley at the mouth of Bear River, struck across to Little River and then followed it down. We were many, many days in getting the boats up this long winding, and ever swifter part of the river. The farther up it we went the more I looked for signs of the enemy, the Blackfeet, and their war brothers, the Big Bellies, but, look as I would, I could never find ever a single footprint that they had made nor any tracks of their horses. I thought that very strange. When we arrived at the mouth of the stream my white chiefs named the Musselshell, some of the men went up it during the afternoon, and, returning, told of a stream coming into it from the plain on the right. My chiefs then told me that it should have my name, as they called it, Sah-ka-já-we-ah.

I asked my man to tell them that I wished they would give it my right name, Bo-í-naiv, Grass Woman.

31

Zebulon Pike

Shortly after Lewis and Clark's expedition was completed,
General James Wilkinson, commander-in-chief of the U.S. Army,
sent the young Zebulon Pike westward, to explore the Arkansas
and Red Rivers. It was a difficult journey and Pike and his group
suffered greatly from the cold. In Colorado the men attempted
unsuccessfully to cross the snow covered mountain that to this
day bears his name — Pike's Peak.

In 1805, Zebulon Pike was dispatched to the Mississippi
River to explore the region and to document Native American
tribes there. A "Bibliographical Sketch" follows.

Source: Mary Gay Humphreys, ed. *The Boys Story of Zebulon M. Pike.* (New
York: Charles Scribner's Sons, 1911), pp. x-xiii, and map.

Zebulon Montgomery Pike, was born at Lamberton, New
Jersey, a suburb of Trenton, January 5, 1779. While a child
his family removed to Bucks County, Pennsylvania, near the
Delaware River, and from thence to Easton. Zebulon Pike is
described as a boy of slender form, very fair, gentle and retiring
in desposition, but of resolute spirit. He had only a common-
school education. One of his teachers was a Mr. Wall, with
whom he studied latin and mathematics. But as his diary shows,
and as his comrades in arms testify, Pike was a student in camp
and on the trail to the end of his days.

....

It was as first lieutenant of the 1st Infantry that Pike was
detailed for detached service, and reported to the head-quarters of
the commanding general at St. Louis, in 1805. This selection

of a young man of twenty-six, for the exploration of the Mississippi River is evidence that his qualities must have attracted attention. At this time there was no definite knowledge of the Louisiana territory, in its northwestern part. President Jefferson had asked of Napoleon the city of New Orleans, and he had received an empire. The area of the United States by the stroke of a pen had been doubled. But instead of spending two millions, Jefferson had spent fifteen millions. Having invested the people's money in this vast territory, it now became necessary to find out what sort of bargain he had made with Napoleon. Lewis and Clark were sent to the Far West, and a second expedition was now organized by the commander-in-chief of the army, General Wilkinson, which was to be strictly military in purpose and method, and to assert the authority of the United States, not only over the unknown Indian tribes of that region, but over the adventurous traders of the Hudson Bay and Northwest Companies.

"In the execution of this voyage," he afterward wrote, "I had no gentleman to aid me, and I literally performed the duties (as far as my limited abilities permitted) of astronomer, surveyor, commanding officer, clerk, spy, hunter, and guide; frequently preceding the party for miles, in order to reconnoiter, and returning in the evening, to sit down in the open air, by firelight to copy the notes, and plot the courses of the day."

The Journals of Zebulon Montgomery Pike

The following excerpts contain Pike's observations of various Native American communities he encountered on his expedition. Pike's 1805 expedition had him exploring the Mississippi River and introducing himself on behalf of the United States government to the Native American communities.

Source: Donald Jackson, ed. *The Journals of Zebulon Montgomery Pike with Letters and Related Documents, Vol. 1.* (University of Oklahoma Press: Norman, 1966), pp. 213-215, 217.

The Minowa Kantongs are the only band of Sioux who use canoes, and by far the most civilized, they being the only ones who have ever built log huts, or cultivated any species of vegetables; and those only a very small quantity of corn and beans; for although I was with them in September or October, I never saw one kettle of either, always using the wild oats for bread. This production nature has furnished to all the most uncultivated nations of the N.W. continent, who may gather a sufficiency in autumn, which, when added to the productions of the chase and the net, ensures them a subsistence through all the seasons of the year. This band is entirely armed with fire arms, but is not considered by the other bands as any thing superior on that account, especially on the plains.

The Washpetong are a roving band; they leave the river St. Peters in the month of April, and do not return from the plains, until the middle of August. Sussitongs of Roche Blanche, have the character of being the most evil disposed Indians, on the river St. Peters. They likewise follow the buffalo in the spring and summer months. Sussitongs of the Lac de Gross Roche (under the Tonnere Rouge) have the character of good hunters and brave warriors, which may principally be attributed to their chief the

Tonnere Rouge, who, at the present day is allowed by both white people and the savages of the different bands, to be (after their own chiefs) the first man in the Sioux nation. The Yanctongs and Titongs are the most independent Indians in the world; they follow the buffalo as chance directs; clothing themselves with the skin, and making their lodges, bridles, and saddles of the same material, the flesh of the animal furnishing their food. Possessing innumerable herds of horses, they are here this day, 500 miles off ten days hence, and find themselves equally at home in either place, moving with a rapidity scarcely to be imagined by the inhabitants of the civilized world.

. . . .

From my knowledge of the Sioux nation, I do not hesitate to pronounce them the most warlike and independent nation of Indians within the boundaries of the United States, their every passion being subservient to that of war; but at the same time, their traders feel themselves perfectly secure of any combination being made against them, but it is extremely necessary to be careful not to injure the honor or feelings of an individual, which is certainly the principal cause of the many broils which occur between them. But never was a trader known to suffer in the estimation of the nation by resenting any indignity offered him; even if it went to taking the life of the offender. Their guttural pronunciation; high cheek bones; their visages, and distinct manners, together with their own traditions, supported by the testimony of neighboring nations, puts in my mind, beyond the shadow of a doubt that they have emigrated from the N.W. point of America, to which they had come across the narrow streights, which in that quarter divides the two continents; and are absolutely descendants of a Tartarean tribe.

. . . .

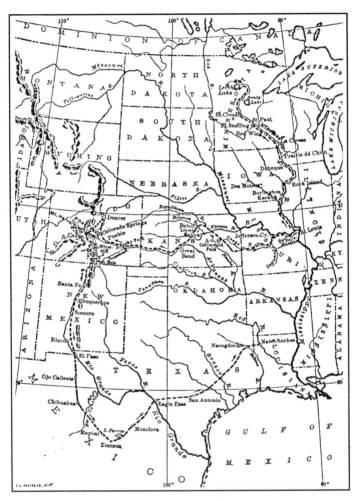

Map of Pike's Explorations. The dotted lines show the routes followed on the several expeditions.

The Chipeways are uncommonly attached to spirituous liquors; but may not this be owing to their traders, who find it much to their interest to encourage their thirst after an article, which enables them to obtain their peltries at so low a rate, as scarcely to be denominated a consideration, and have reduced the people near the establishments, to a degree of degradation unparalleled? The Algonquin language is one of the most copious and sonorous languages of all the savage dialects in North America; and is spoken and understood by the various nations (except the Sioux) from the Gulf of St. Lawrence to Lake Winipie.

This nation is much more mild and docile than the Sioux; and (if we may judge from unprejudiced observers) more cool and deliberate in action; but the latter possess a much higher sense of the *honor of their nation:* the others *plan for self-preservation.* The Sioux attack with impetuosity, the other defends with every necessary precaution. But the superior number of the Sioux, would have enabled them to have annihilated the Chipeways long since, had it not been for the nature of their country, which entirely precludes the possibility of an attack on horseback. Also, gives them a decided advantage over an enemy, who, being half armed with arrows, the least twig of a bush would turn the shaft of death out of its direction. Whereas, the whizzing bullet holds its course, nor spends its force short of the destined victim. Thus, we generally have found, that, when engaged in a Prairie the Sioux came off victorious; but if in the woods, even, if not obliged to retreat, the carcases of their slaughtered brethren shew how dearly they purchase the victory.

The Mountain Men:
Scouts, Trappers, and Traders

*Between 1810 and 1840 many entered the commercial side
of scouting in the West. Others, motivated by the desire to gain
tremendous personal wealth, became trappers and fur traders.
The abundance of wildlife in the West brought eager mountain
men to the Great Lakes Region and far to the Northwest, beyond
the Rocky Mountains. Large fur trade markets grew in St.
Louis, Missouri, and Taos, New Mexico, where trappers sold
their pelts to be shipped East and to Europe.*

*Many of the men involved in scouting and trapping were
especially valued for their knowledge of the western terrain and
were often employed as scouts to the hundreds of settlers moving
West. Their adventures and misadventures have become part of
America's great folklore of the West.*

John Colter: Explorer and Scout

John Colter, a thirty-year-old Virginian who had accompanied Lewis and Clark on their expedition west, became one
of the most accomplished early trappers and scouts. Leaving the
"Corps of Discovery" expedition team in 1806, Colter served
as a guide for two trappers for a short time, and then worked
for a prominent and unscrupulous fur trader named Manuel Lisa.
Lisa sent him on a mission to the Crow Indian Nation, from
Ft. Raymond, Wyoming. Colter journeyed on foot in the
mountains of what is now Montana, Idaho, and Wyoming. It
was Colter who, although warned by the Crow of evil spirits,

ventured into the uninhabited land, which is now known as Yellowstone National Park. With its bubbling hot springs and amazing 150-foot geysers, Colter's reports of the area were not believed upon his return to Ft. Raymond. People referred to his tales of this unusual wilderness area as "Colter's Hell." Although Colter had survived incredible encounters with nature and with the Native Americans, he could not survive a case of jaundice. Colter died from it in Missouri at the age of 38.

James P. Beckwourth:
African American Trapper and Scout

Although very little has been written about black trappers, scouts, and traders, African Americans were contributors to the exploration and expansion of the west. Jim Beckwourth was a Virginia-born mulatto who spent time as a trapper and a gold prospector during the Colorado gold rush of 1859. He is credited with exploring a pass (which is named after him) through the Sierra-Nevada Mountains to the gold fields of California.

Because of his dark coloring, Beckwourth was sometimes mistaken for an Indian. He felt at home with the Native Americans he met, and spent seven years (1826-1833) living in the Crow Nation. He married at least one chief's daughter, and eventually became a Crow Chief. In 1846, Beckwourth acted as a scout in the Mexican War.

✧✧✧✧✧

John Jacob Astor: Fur Trader

This excerpt contains a discussion of John Jacob Astor,
founder of the American Fur Company, and an active player in
the Northwest American fur trade.

Source: Ripley Hitchcock. *The Louisiana Purchase and the Exploration Early History and Building of the West.* (Boston: Ginn and Co., The Athenaeum Press, 1904), pp. 227-229.

Of the many adventurous journeys to the vague western
boundaries of Louisiana and beyond, the most remarkable for
the first decade of the American fur trade was the expedition of
Wilson Price Hunt, leader of the "overland Astorians." This
expedition was due to the commercial enterprise of John Jacob
Astor. The journey of Lewis and Clark had shown that the
upper Missouri and the country beyond the mountains was rich
in furs. Mr. Astor saw a tempting opportunity for trading posts
from the mouth of the Columbia to its source and along the
Missouri, an opportunity which offered not only trade with our
East but a most profitable commerce with China and Japan.
In a word, this German "captain of industry" saw a practicable
northwest passage, — a possible means of reaching that rich
Oriental trade which had tempted the voyages of Columbus and
of later seekers for a route to the Spice Islands and Cathay.

In 1808 Mr. Astor organized the American Fur Company,
and later the Pacific Fur Company, the latter merely a name
for the branch of the first company which was to operate on the
Pacific coast. Two expeditions were planned, one to go by sea
and one by land. The ship carrying the former left New York in
1810, reaching the mouth of the Columbia the following spring.
The foundation of Astoria was accomplished under unfortunate
auspices, and the result was a failure that need not be dwelt upon,

since our present concern lies with Hunt's overland journey, which may be said to have opened the Oregon trail.

In March, 1811, Hunt left St. Louis with his party and ascended the Missouri. His original purpose was to continue up the Missouri and the Yellowstone. But tidings of hostile Blackfeet on the route induced him to leave the river at the country of the Arikaras, thirteen hundred and twenty-five miles above the mouth of the Missouri, and to make the journey by land. His party, sixty-four in number, turned westward into an unknown country. They passed near the Black Hills, and made their way through the Big Horn and Wind River mountains to the valley of Green River. Thence they crossed the divide to the Snake River, and after many bitter experiences in the mountain winter they reached the Columbia late in January, 1812, and on February 15 arrived in Astoria.

This journey occupied three hundred and forty days, and the distance according to Hunt's estimate was thirty-five hundred miles. That summer there was sent back from Astoria a party which, owing to various blunders, spent nearly as long a time on its return journey, so that it was nearly two years before news of Hunt reached St. Louis. These two expeditions showed the way to Oregon. But various mistakes in management, the war with Great Britain, and the approach of an English war vessel resulted in the abandonment of Astoria and the end of Mr. Astoria's dream of a northwest trading route to the Orient.

Francis Parkman: Trapper on the Oregon Trail

*Shortly after Francis Parkman graduated from Harvard in
1844, he made plans to explore the West with friend and fellow
Bostonian, Quincy Adams Shaw, and record his experiences for
publication. The following excerpt from Parkman's journal of
his trip in 1846 focuses on his observation of a trapper. The
journal as a whole presents an eye-witness account of his encounters with Indians, emigrant families, outlaws, scouts, and
Mormons whom he met along the Oregon Trail. The names
mentioned in the text below refer to French Canadian trappers
(Rouleau and Saraphin).*

Source: Francis Parkman. *The Journals of Francis Parkman.* (First published
in 1849, *The Oregon Trail* by Francis Parkman. New American Library, N.Y.,
1950), pp. 185-187.

Like other trappers, Rouleau's life was one of contrast and
variety. It was only at certain seasons, and for a limited time,
that he was absent on his expeditions. For the rest of the year
he would lounge about the fort, or encamp with his friends in
its vicinity, hunting, or enjoying all the luxury of inaction; but
when once in pursuit of the beaver, he was involved in extreme
privations and perils. Hand and foot, eye and ear, must be always
alert. Frequently he must content himself with devouring his
evening meal uncooked, lest the light of his fire should attract
the eyes of some wandering Indian; and sometimes having made
his rude repast, he must leave his fire still blazing, and with-
draw to a distance under cover of the darkness, that his disap-
pointed enemy, drawn thither by the light, may find his victim
gone, and be unable to trace his footsteps in the gloom. This
is the life led by scores of men among the Rocky Mountains.
I once met a trapper whose breast was marked with the scars of

six bullets and arrows, one of his arms broken by a shot and one of his knees shattered; yet still, with the mettle of New England, whence he had come, he continued to follow his perilous calling.

On the last day of our stay in this camp, the trappers were ready for departure. When in the Black Hills they had caught seven beavers, and they now left their skins in charge of Reynal, to be kept until their return. Their strong, gaunt horses were equipped with rusty Spanish bits, and rude Mexican saddles, to which wooden stirrups were attached, while a buffalo-robe was rolled up behind, and a bundle of beaver-traps slung at the pommel. These, together with their rifles, knives, powder-horns and bullet-pouches, flint and steel and a tin cup, composed their whole travelling equipment. They shook hands with us, and rode away; Saraphin, with his grim countenance, was in advance; but Rouleau, clambering gayly into his seat, kicked his horse's sides, flourished his whip, and trotted briskly over the prairie, trolling forth a Canadian song at the top of his voice. Reynal looked after them with his face of brutal selfishness.

"Well," he said, "if they are killed, I shall have the beaver. They'll fetch me fifty dollars at the fort, anyhow."

This was the last I saw of them.

We had been five days in the hunting-camp, and the meat, which all this time had hung drying in the sun, was not fit for transportation. Buffalo-hides also had been procured in sufficient quantities for making the next season's lodges; but it remained to provide the long poles on which they were to be supported. These were only to be had among the tall spruce woods of the Black Hills, and in that direction therefore our next move was to be made. Amid the general abundance which during this time had prevailed in the camp, there were no instances of individual privation; for although the hide and the tongue of the buffalo belong by exclusive right to the hunter who has killed it, yet any one else is equally entitled to help himself from the rest of the carcass. Thus the weak, the aged, and even the indolent come in for a share of the spoils, and many a helpless old woman, who would otherwise perish from starvation, is sustained in abundance.

Daniel Boone and Davy Crockett

*When the United States was a young struggling country,
Americans praised hard work, honesty, and adventure. These
values helped shape our nation. Daniel Boone and Davy Crockett
lived their lives by these rules. As they helped build the new
west, their adventures contributed to the ever-growing popularity
of legends and folktales.*

*There were many similarities in the lives of Daniel Boone
and Davy Crockett. They were both raised on farms in the back-
woods country. Boone grew up in what is now western Pennsylvania, and Crockett was raised in Green County, Tennessee.
Both learned to live off the land, and could hunt, trap, scout, and
track as well as any Native American. In fact, they learned many
of their skills from Native Americans. Unlike many people at
that time, Boone and Crockett were tolerant and sympathetic to
the plight of the indigenous people, who lived on the land long
before the white men arrived.*

Daniel Boone

Daniel Boone helped cut the first road across the Cumberland
Gap to Kentucky. Following small trails used by Native Americans and trappers, Boone and his crew chopped down trees and
removed rocks and other debris, creating a wilderness road near
the intersection of Tennessee, Virginia, and Kentucky. In 1775,
Boone lead the earliest group of settlers across the Appalachian
Mountains into Kentucky. By the turn of the century, over
3,000 travelers used the road as they journeyed West. In 1775,
Boone also helped build a fort and founded Boonesborough, one
of the first organized settlements in Kentucky.

Daniel Boone wore pants and shirts made of buckskin and moccasins of deerskin.

Davy Crockett

Although Davy Crockett had a family and a farm in Tennessee, he was filled with a sense of adventure and often took off to the woods for weeks at a time. He lived off the land, searching for new trails and spending time with his Native American friends. In 1827, Crockett was elected to the United States Congress to represent Tennessee. People called him the "Coonskin Congressman," and the "man of the people." In Congress, Crockett fought for the rights of the common man and continued to voice his support for the rights of Native Americans. Crockett fought in many battles, and, in 1836, died fighting at the Alamo in Texas.

The "Crockett Almanacs"

In 1835, a series of pamphlets called the "Crockett Almanacks" was published about Boone, Crockett, and other western folk heroes. The Almanacs were similar to today's comic books. They contained sketches and adventure stories about the latest exploits of western heroes. Legends about Boone and Crockett killing bears with their bare hands, learning to shoot before they would walk, outrunning deer, and whittling boats out of tree stumps were common tales. People had great fun spinning yarns about "Old Tick Licker," and "Old Betsy," the names Boone and Crockett gave to their rifles. Their adventures and accomplishments were woven into tall tales and retold often during long winter nights.

Source: Franklin J. Meine, ed., *The Crockett Almanacks Nashville Series, 1835-1838.* (The Caxton Club, Chicago, 1955), pp. 45-47.

Vol.1.] " *Go Ahead.* " [No.2.

Davy Crockett's
ALMANACK,
OF WILD SPORTS IN THE WEST,
And Life in the Backwoods.

CALCULATED FOR ALL THE STATES IN THE UNION.

1836

Col. Crockett's Method of Wading the Mississippi.

NASHVILLE, TENN. PUBLISHED FOR THE AUTHOR.

49

Crockett's Fight with a Cat-fish

There is one of my young scrapes that has never yet appeared in print, and I think I might as well give it to the reader in this place.

I cut out one morning to go over the Mississippi on business that concerns nobody but myself. I shoved off my canoe and had paddled into the middle of the stream, when a monstratious great Cat-Fish, better known by the name of a Mississippi Lawyer, came swimming along close under the bows of my boat. I tied a rope around my middle, at one end of it was a fishing spear, and I soon got a chance to dart it into the varmint. He run and I hauled, and it whirled my canoe round and round like a car-wheel on a railroad. I concluded to stand up to my rack, and I couldn't very well help it, seeing that one end of the rope was made fast to my middle. At last on account of his giving one end of the line a tremendous kick with his tail, and partly on account of the canoe slipping away from under me, I went souse into the water. The cat-fish at the same time seized the slack of my breeches with his teeth and tore them clear off me. I didn't care much for that, as it was easier swimming without them. So I drew out my knife, and when the fish came up and made a pass at my throat with his open mouth, I stabbed out one of his eyes. That made him plunge, but as he was going down I grabbed him by the tail, and went down with him till I touched bottom with one foot. All this time the spear remained in the plaguy varmint, and while under water, I come across a sawyer that was sticking up; I took a turn with my line around the sawyer, and the fish was brought up all standing. So he come at me again, and I manoeuvred to get on the blind side of him — but he could see better under water than I could, though he had but one eye, and he turned short upon me just as I was about stabbing him to

the heart. I then clinched right round his body, and rammed one arm down his throat, while I tried to stab him with the other hand — then I tell you the fire flew, I never see a fellow kick, bite and scratch as he did. I had been under water a pretty good long while, and there was a ringing in my ears that warned me to finish my job as soon as I could. "I tell you there's no quarter to be given," said I to the fish, perceiving him to grow a little faintish. With that he fell to fighting again, and I believe he would have scratched my bones bare, if I had not got a chance to shove my knife to the hilt in his belly. I then cut my line, and rose to the surface pretty well fagged out. Arter I had rested a spell, I dove down and tied a line to the fish and hauled up his corpse. It measured twelve feet in length.

"Davy Crockett"

These are three verses of a song written about Davy Crockett.
The author, R.R. Brown, wrote the song in England about 1833.
Davy Crockett's popularity was world renown.

From old Kentuck I'm newly come
A Hundred Horse pow'r CRETUR
The Yellow forest flow'r so rum,
Half Horse half Alligator
Perhaps the queerist chap you've seed
With Spirits no one higher
There's no back out about the
Breed Of Colonel Nimrod Wildfire

My weight in wild Cats I have whipp'd
'Tis true and never blunder'd
or I'll be curry-comb'd when stripp'd
By just A even hundred
In a Cast Iron pot I'll quick fly
Up fam'd Niagara's fall Sir
Or be just Te-to-taciouslly
Exflunkefied — that's all Sir.

In Kentucky all's great and grand
A Cock-boat there's a steamer
My sweetheart shot a Bear off hand
She's what I call a Screamer,
The Sun so bright, the Moon so pale
SUSPOSE, I'm no Astrologer,
Are there on the high-pressure Scale
I call that a Sock-dologer.

Other Voices from the West

The following is a narrative on frontier life written by James Hall in 1828.

Source: James Hall. *Letters From the West: Containing Sketches of Scenery, Manners, and Customs; and Anecdotes Connected with the First Settlements of the Western Sections of the United States,* 1828. (Scholars' Facsimiles & Reprints, Gainesville, Florida, 1967), pp. 288-290.

Kentucky was settled at a period when religious fanaticism had vanished, and when the principles of the revolution, then in full operation, had engendered liberal and original modes of thinking — when every man was a politician, a soldier, and a patriot, ready to make war or to make laws, to put his hand to the plough or to the helm of state, as circumstances might require. They went to the wilderness with all these new notions in their heads, full of ardour, and full of projects, determined to add a new state to the family of republics, at all hazards. With Boon for their file-leader, they resolutely breasted all opposition. The rifle and the axe were incessantly employed. The savage was to be expelled; the panther, the wolf, and the bear to be exterminated; the forest to be razed; houses to be built: and when all this was accomplished, their labours were but commenced. Separated, by an immense wilderness, and by the rugged ridges of the Alleghany mountains, from the older settlements, the transportation of heavy articles was at first impossible, and for many years difficult and expensive. The pioneers, therefore, brought little else with them than their weapons, and their ammunition; those who followed in their footsteps brought cattle, and hogs, and a few articles of immediate necessity, laden upon pack-horses. With no tools but an axe and an augur, the settler built his cabin; with a chimney built of sticks, and a door hung upon wooden hinges, and confined with a wooden latch. Chairs, tables, and bedsteads, were fabricated with the same unwieldy tools. These primitive dwellings are by no means so wretched as their name and their rude workmanship seem to imply. They still constitute the usual residence of the farmers in new settlements, and I have often found them roomy, tight, and comfortable. If one cabin is not sufficient, another, and another is added, until the whole family is accommodated; and thus the homestead of a substantial farmer often resembles a little village. Farming utensils were next to be fabricated, and land to be cleared and fenced; and while all this was carrying on, the new settler had to provide food for his family with his rifle, to look after his stock, which ranged the woods, exposed to the "wild varmints," and to "keep a red eye out" for Indians. In addition to these more important matters, it will readily be imagined, that a number of little things would have to be made, and done, and provided, before the woodsman, adhering strictly to the system of *home manufacture*, could be "*well fixed*," as their phrase is; a man who goes into the woods, as one of these veterans observed to me, "has a *heap* of little *fixens* to *study out*, and a great deal of *projecking* to do, as well as hard work."

Dr. Dodderidge's Observations
on the Life of Early Settlers

*The following excerpt is from the writing of a frontier settler
named Dr. Dodderidge. He writes about his observations on the
life of early settlers.*

Source: James Hall. *Sketches of History, Life, and Manners, in the West.*
(Philadelphia: Harrison Hall, 1835), pp. 218-219, 293.

He says, "some of the early settlers took the precaution to
come over the mountains in the spring, leaving their families
behind to raise a crop of corn, and then return and bring them
out in the fall. This I should think was the better way. Others,
especially those whole families were small, brought them with
them in the spring. My father took the latter course. His family
was but small, and he brought them all with him. The Indian
meal which he brought over the mountains, was expended six
weeks too soon, so that for that length of time we had to live
without bread. The lean venison, and the breast of wild turkeys,
we were taught to call bread. The flesh of the bear was denominated meat. This artifice did not succeed very well; after living in
this way for some time, we became sickly; the stomach seemed
to be always empty, and tormented with a sense of hunger. I
remember how narrowly the children watched the growth of the
potato tops, pumpkin and squash vines, hoping from day to day
to get something to answer in the place of bread. How delicious
was the taste of the young potatoes when we got them! What a
jubilee when we were permitted to pull the young corn for roast-
ing ears! Still more so, when it had acquired sufficient hardness
to be made into johnny cakes, by the aid of a tin grater. We then
became healthy, vigorous, and contented with our situation, poor
as it was."

"The furniture of the table, for several years after the settlement of this country, consisted of a few pewter dishes, plates, and spoons, but mostly of wooden bowls, trenchers, and noggins. If these last were scarce, gourds and hard shelled squashes made up the deficiency. The iron pots, knives and forks, were brought from the east side of the mountains, along with salt and iron, on pack-horses."

In the following excerpt, Hall writes about the importance of hunting to frontier settlers.

Hunting was an important part of the employment of the early settlers. For some years after their emigration, the forest supplied them with a greater part of their subsistence; some families were without bread for months at a time, and it often happened that the first meal of the day could not be prepared until the hunter returned with the spoils of the chase. Fur and peltry were the circulating medium of the country; the hunter had nothing else to give in exchange for rifles, salt, lead, and iron. Hunting, therefore, was the employment, rather than the sport, of the pioneers — yet it was pursued with the alacrity and sense of enjoyment which attends an exciting and favourite amusement. Dangerous and fatiguing as are its vicissitudes, those who become accustomed to the chase, generally retain through life their fondness for the rifle.

Mrs. Rowan's Courage

The following excerpt tells about the courage of a mother during an attack on her family by hostile Native Americans. The family was travelling by boat down the Ohio River.

Source: John Frost, LL. D. *Pioneer Mothers of the West; or Daring and Heroic Deeds of American Women.* (Boston: Lee and Shepard, 1869), 65-67.

In the following narrative, communicated by John Rowan, of Kentucky, to Dr. Drake, of Cincinnati, we have an account of a display of cool courage by a woman, in a degree rarely witnessed, even in the west.

Settlers often travelled the Ohio River in flatboats, which could transport their livestock as well as their belongings.

In the latter part of April, 1784, my father with his family, and five other families, set out from Louisville, in two flat-bottomed boats, for the Long Falls of Green river. The intention was to descend the Ohio river to the mouth of Green river, and ascend that river to the place of destination. At that time there were no settlements in Kentucky, within one hundred miles of Long Falls of the Green river (afterwards called Vienna.) The families were in one boat and their cattle in the other. When we had descended the river Ohio, about one hundred miles, and were near the middle of it, gliding along very securely, as we thought, about ten o'clock at night, we heard a prodigious yelling, by Indians, some two or three miles below us, on the northern shore. We had floated but a little distance farther down the river, when we saw a number of fires on that shore. The yelling still continued, and we concluded that they had captured a boat which had passed us about midday, and were massacreing their captives. Our two boats were lashed together, and the best practical arrangements were made for defending them. The men were distributed by my father to the best advantage in case of an attack; they were seven in number, including himself. The boats were neared to the Kentucky shore, with as little noise from the oars as possible. We were afraid to approach too near the Kentucky shore, lest there might be Indians on that shore also. We had not yet reached their uppermost fire, (their fires were extended along the bank at intervals for half a mile or more,) and we entertained a faint hope that we might slip by unperceived. But they discovered us when we had got about midway of their fires, and commanded us to come to. We were silent, for my father had given strict orders that no one should utter any sound but that of the rifle: and not that until the Indians should come within powder burning distance. They united in a most terrific yell, and rushed to their canoes, and pursued us. We floated on in silence — not an oar was pulled. They approached us within a hundred yards, with a seeming determination to board us. Just at this moment my mother rose from her seat, collected the axes, and placed one by the side of each man, where he stood with his gun, touching him on the knee with the handle of the axe, as she leaned it up by him against the side of the boat, to let him know it was there, and retired to her seat, retaining a hatchet for herself. The Indians continued hovering on our rear, and yelling, for near three miles, when, awed by the inference which they drew from our silence, they relinquished farther pursuit. None but those who have had a practical acquaintance with Indian warfare, can form a just idea of the terror which this hideous yelling is calculated to inspire. I was then about ten years old, and shall never forget the sensations of that night; nor can I ever cease to admire the fortitude and composure displayed by my mother on that trying occasion. We were saved, I have no doubt, by the judicious system of conduct and defence, which my father had prescribed to our little band. We were seven men and three boys — but nine guns in all. They were more than a hundred. My mother, in speaking of it afterwards, in her calm way, said, "We had made a providential escape, for which we ought to feel grateful."

That mother of the west should have a monument. It would remind her descendants who are accustomed to hearing females designated as the "weaker vessels," that upon trying occasions, the strength of soul, which is beyond that of sinew and muscle, has appeared in woman, and may appear again.

Timeline

1763	British Proclamation of 1763. Forbade colonists from settling on the frontier.
1775	Daniel Boone blazes a trail through the Cumberland Gap. Boonesborough founded in Kentucky. American Revolution begins.
1783	American Revolution ends. Land protected by the Proclamation of 1763 now belongs to the United States.
1795	Spain signs a three-year treaty with the United States that permits Americans to deposit their trade goods at the Port of New Orleans.
1800	Thomas Jefferson becomes President.
1803	The United States purchases Louisiana Province from France.
1804	The Lewis and Clark expedition begins.
1805	The Zebulon M. Pike expedition begins.
1808	John J. Astor organizes the American Fur Company.
1826- *1833*	Jim Beckwourth lives with the Crow.
1827	Davy Crockett elected to the U.S. Congress.
1835	"Crockett Almanacks" are published.
1846	Francis Parkman journeys on the Oregon Trail.

Definitions

carcases   The bodies of dead animals.

cutlash   A small swordlike weapon used for self defense in the early nineteenth century.

flora   A general word for plant life.

fauna   A general word for animal life.

noggins   A small mug that one would use for a hot beverage.

peltries   A collective name for animal skins.

portage   Transporting boats, goods or people from one waterway to another.

small pox   A highly contagious disease that was spread by a virus and caused an eruption of pox on the skin.

varmint   A word that describes any person or animal that likes to cause trouble.

Suggested Further Reading

Burt, Olive. *Sacajawea.* New York: Franklin Watts, 1978.

Cantor, George. "Touring the Black Past," p. 38. *Legacy, A Supplement to American Heritage,* February 1995.

Cavan, Seamus. *Daniel Boone and the Opening of the Ohio Country.* New York: Chelsea House Publishers, 1991.

Collins, James L. *Exploring the American West.* New York: Franklin Watts, 1989.

Deer, Mark. *The Frontiersman: The Real Life and Many Legends of Davy Crockett.* New York: William Morrow & Co., 1993.

Fitz-Gerald, Christine. *The World's Great Explorers — Merriwether Lewis and William Clark.* Chicago: Childrens Press, 1991.

Hargrove, Jim. *Daniel Boone Pioneer Trailblazer.* Chicago: Childrens Press, 1985.

Neuberger, Richard. *The Lewis and Clark Expedition.* New York: Random House, 1951.

Phelan, Mary Kay. *The Story of the Louisiana Purchase.* New York: Thomas Y. Crowell, 1979.

Stallones, Jared. *Zebulon Pike and the Explorers of the American Southwest.* New York: Chelsea House Publishers, 1992.

Townsend, Tom. *Davy Crockett.* Austin, Texas: Eakin Press, 1987.

Also Note:

Cobblestone: The History Magazine for Young People, by Cobblestone Publishing, Peterborough, NH, Sept. 1980 issue "The Lewis and Clark Expedition, 1804-1806," June 1988 issue "Daniel Boone."

About the Editor

Cheryl Edwards has degrees in history and anthropology from Michigan State University. She and her husband Jon spent two years doing archival research in London, Rome, Paris, and Brussells for Jon's doctoral thesis on Ethiopian history. While working in London's Public Records Office, Cheryl indexed 550 volumes of court records kept by the British in Addis Ababa, Ethiopia. "I have always enjoyed reading old documents and trying to figure out what shaped people's thoughts and actions. Historians are very much like detectives. It is their job to find primary sources, and interpret them."

As a teacher, Cheryl taught history and writing to students in Ohio, Michigan, and New Hampshire. Cheryl has been a free-lance writer since 1985. She lives with her husband, Jon, and her two sons, Aaron, age six, and Neil, age three, in Pennington, New Jersey.

The Perspectives on History Series